Janice VanCleave's

Play and Find Out

about

Bugs

Easy Experiments for Young Children

John Wiley & Sons, Inc.

New York • Chichester • Weinheim • Brisbane • Singapore • Toronto

Published by John Wiley & Sons, Inc.
Published simultaneously in Canada.

The publisher and the author have made every reasonable effort to ensure that the experiments and activities in this book are safe when conducted as instructed but assume no responsibility for any damage caused or sustained while performing the experiments or activities in the book. Parents, guardians, and/or teachers should supervise young readers who undertake the experiments and activities in this book.

Library of Congress Cataloging-in-Publication Data

VanCleave, Janice Pratt.
    [Play and find out about bugs]
    Janice VanCleave's play and find out about bugs : easy experiments for young children / Janice VanCleave.
        p.   cm. — (Play and find out series)
    Includes index.
    Summary: Presents simple experiments answering such questions about insects as "Are spiders insects?" "Where do butterflies come from?" and "Why do fireflies light up?"
    ISBN 0-471-17664-8 (cloth : alk. paper).—ISBN 0-471-17663-X (pbk. : alk. paper)
    1. Insects—Experiments—Juvenile literature. [1. Insects—Experiments. 2. Spiders—Experiments. 3. Experiments. 4. Questions and answers.] I. Title. II. Series: VanCleave, Janice Pratt. Play and find out series.
QL468.5.V34 1998
595.7—dc21
                                          97-52088

Dedication

This book is dedicated to a special teacher whom I proudly call my friend. She is a very conscientious worker. Who but Laura Fields Roberts would take experiments along on a bicycle vacation in order to complete her reviews of the experiments in this book to meet my deadline? With campground picnic tables as her desks, she finished the work and even took time to add special notes about insects flying and crawling around in that area. I am always thankful that the Lord brought Laura into my life.

Acknowledgments

I wish to express my appreciation to Donna Kelly Duncan, principal of St. Matthews Elementary School in Jefferson County Public Schools in Louisville, Kentucky. Because of Ms. Duncan's approval and support, the following students at St. Matthews, under the direction of Laura Roberts and her coworker Sandra Williams Petrey, tested the activities in this book: Cameron Abell, Morgan Baker, Sean Cummings, Matthew Dowell, Morgan Everett, Emily Ferry, Courtney Gilliam, Elsha Gross, Jordan Hincks, Tate Houchens, Whitney Johnson, Spencer Jordan, Joseph Moss, Andrew Payne, Denitra Reed, Caroline Schmidt, Brittiany Skinner, Taylor Sowards, Wesley Stewart, Chie Togami, John Tucker, Steven Vance, Jacob Whalin, and Jennifer Woods.

A special thank you goes to Anne Skrabanek and her children, Sarah, Benjamin, and Rebecca. This group of science explorers spent a great deal of time not only testing the experiments for this book, but also doing field research.

My grandchildren are faithful helpers. These dedicated science explorers are Kimberly, Jennifer, David, and Davin VanCleave and Lauren and Lacey Russell. I do so appreciate their support and willingness while assisting me in this project, even when it included riding in a car with collected bugs both dead and alive. What fun it was to be part of the discoveries they made while Playing and Finding Out about Bugs.

As always, my husband, Wade, patiently lived through the research and writing of this book. All bugs inside and out were considered part of the project and were caught and studied. Spiders had a free rein to spin their webs when and where they pleased. Wade is a real science trooper, but he has suggested the next book be about things with fewer or no legs—fish maybe.

Contents

Dear Friends,

Welcome to science playtime!

The scientific play activities in this book are about bugs. Young children generally love bugs, and are excited to learn about them. Real bugs are used in some of the experiments, but only if the bugs are harmless. Even when bugs are not used, expect your child to be delighted by models of such things as fireflies that glow like a camping light stick.

Discovering things on their own gives kids a wonderful feeling of success. All they need is your friendly guidance, a few good ideas, and their natural curiosity. This book is full of fun ideas. It contains instructions for more than 50 simple, hands-on experiments inspired by questions from real kids. While you play together, your child will find out the answer to questions such as "Do bugs have teeth?" "How high can bugs jump?" and lots of other things that children wonder about.

So get ready to enter into a science adventure.

Playfully yours,

Janice VanCleave

Before You Begin

1 **_Read the experiment completely before starting._** When possible, practice the experiment by yourself prior to your science playtime. This increases your understanding of the topic and makes you more familiar with the procedure and the materials. If you know the experiment well, it will be easier for you to give your child instructions and answer questions. For more information about the basic science behind each experiment, see the Appendix.

2 **_Select a place to work._** The kitchen table is usually the best place for the experiments. It provides space and access to an often needed water supply.

3 **_Choose a time._** There is no best time to play with your child, and play should be the main point when doing the experiments in this book. Select a time when you will have the fewest distractions so that you can complete the experiment. If your family has a schedule, you may allot a specific amount of time for the experiment. You may want to set an exact starting time so that the child can watch the clock and become more familiar with time. Try to schedule 5 to 10 minutes at the close of each session to have everyone clean up.

4 **_Collect supplies._** You will have less frustration and more fun if all the materials are ready before you start. (See "Tips on Materials" in the box on the next page.)

5 ***Do not rush through the experiment.*** Follow each step carefully, and for sure and safe results, never skip steps or add your own. Safety is of the utmost importance, and it is a good technique to teach children to follow instructions when doing an experiment.

Tips on Materials

- Some experiments call for water. If you want everything to be at the worktable, you can supply water in a pitcher or soda bottle.
- Extra paper towels are always handy for accidental spills, especially if the experiment calls for liquids. A large bowl can be used for waste liquids, and the bowl can be emptied in the sink later.
- To save time, you can precut some of the materials (except string; see below).
- Do not cut string in advance, because it generally gets tangled and is difficult to separate. You and the child can measure and cut the string together.
- You may want to keep labeled shoe boxes filled with basic materials that are used in many experiments, such as scissors, tape, marking pens, and so forth.

- The specific sizes and types of paper or other listed materials are those used when these experiments were tested. This doesn't mean that substituting a different type of material will result in a failed experiment. Substitution of materials should be a value judgment made after you have read an experiment to determine the use of the material. For example, you could replace an index card with a stiff piece of paper of comparable suggested size.
- For large groups, multiply the material by the number in the group so that each person can perform the experiment individually. Some of the materials (like glue) can be shared, so read the procedure ahead of time to determine quantities.

6 ***Have fun!*** Don't worry if the child isn't "getting" the science principle, or if the results aren't exactly perfect. If you feel the results are too different from those described, reread the instructions and start over from step 1.

7 ***Enjoy the wonder of participating in the learning process.*** Remember, it is OK for your child not to discover the scientific explanation. For example, when you perform the experiment "Springy," the child may be too excited about testing his flea hopper to stop and listen to your explanation of why fleas jump so high. Don't force the child to listen. Join in the fun and make a magic moment to remember. Later, when questions about jumping bugs arise, you can remind the child of the fun time that you had doing the "Springy" experiment, then repeat the experiment, providing the explanation.

Collecting

I.D.

Round Up These Things

your pointer finger

Later You'll Need

lemon-size ball of modeling clay
round toothpick
scissors
three 12-inch (30-cm) chenille craft stems (available at craft stores) or pipe cleaners
tissue paper
pencil
transparent tape
two 7-mm wiggle eyes

Look at the pictures of Bugsy, the cartoon insect. Count the different body parts that Bugsy is pointing to with the ends of his legs. Say the names of the different parts with Bugsy as you touch them. Bugsy has three body parts: the head, the thorax, and the abdomen.

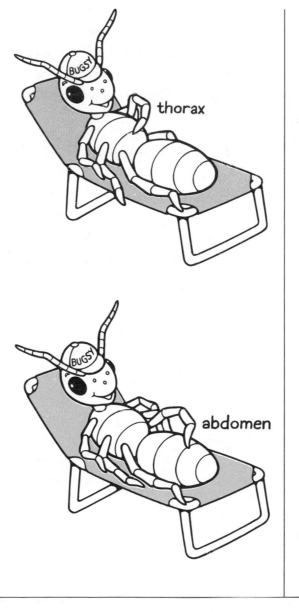

thorax

abdomen

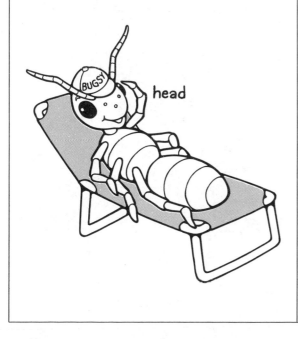

head

2 How many legs does Bugsy have? Touch each leg as you count them. There are six legs, which equals three pairs of legs. His legs are all connected to his middle body part, the thorax.

So Now We Know

Not all creepy-crawlies are insects. You can recognize insects by using the 3 + 3 rule. This rule means that an insect has three body parts and three pairs of legs.

More Fun Things to Know and Do

Most insects have two antennae to feel with and two or four wings. Here's a way to make a model of an insect with two antennae and four wings:

- Form 3 balls—small, medium, and large—from the clay.

- Break the toothpick in half and stick half of each piece into either end of the medium-size piece of clay.

- Push the balls of clay together, with the medium-size ball in the center. The small ball of clay is the head, the middle ball is the thorax, and the large ball is the abdomen.

head   thorax   abdomen

- ADULT STEP   Cut each of the craft stems in half, then cut each piece in half again to make 12 equal-size pieces.

- Use 6 of the stems to make legs. Do this by pushing about ½ inch (1.25 cm) of each stem into the clay, 3 legs in each side of the thorax. Bend each leg as shown.

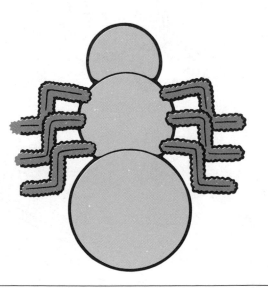

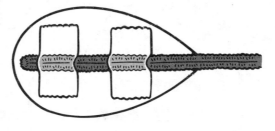

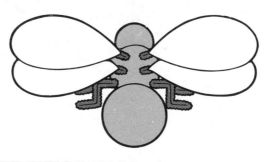

- Lay the tissue paper over the wing pattern shown. Trace the wing using the pencil.

  wing pattern

- Repeat the previous step to trace 4 wings.

- ADULT STEP   Cut out the 4 wings from the tissue paper.

- Tape 1 craft stem to each wing as shown.

- Stick 2 wings into each side of the thorax above the legs by pushing the end of each craft stem into the clay. The front wings should overlap the hind wings.

- Press the eyes into the clay, one on each side of the head.

- Use the remaining 2 craft stems to make antennae by pushing them slightly into the head between the eyes. Bend the tips of the stems as shown.

Trapper

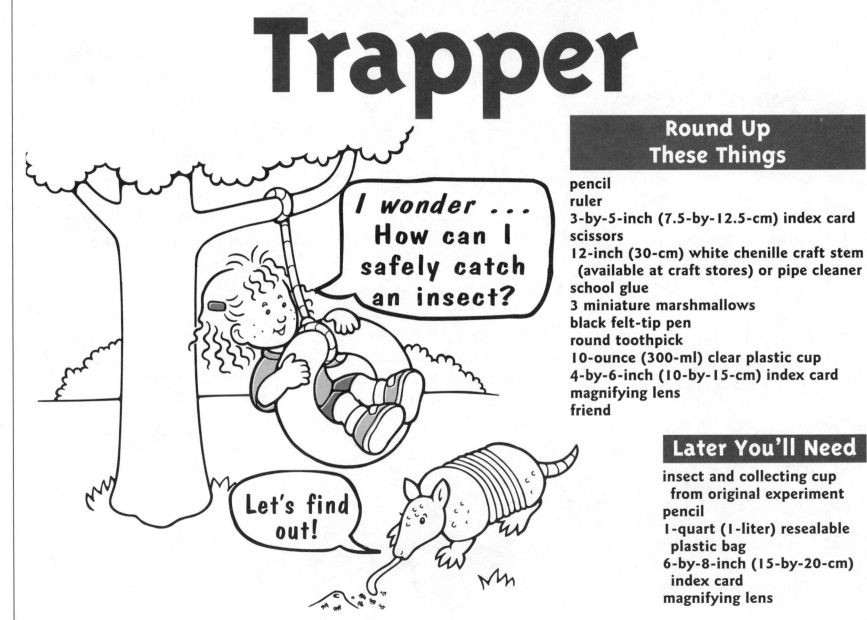

I wonder . . . How can I safely catch an insect?

Let's find out!

Round Up These Things

pencil
ruler
3-by-5-inch (7.5-by-12.5-cm) index card
scissors
12-inch (30-cm) white chenille craft stem
  (available at craft stores) or pipe cleaner
school glue
3 miniature marshmallows
black felt-tip pen
round toothpick
10-ounce (300-ml) clear plastic cup
4-by-6-inch (10-by-15-cm) index card
magnifying lens
friend

Later You'll Need

insect and collecting cup
  from original experiment
pencil
1-quart (1-liter) resealable
  plastic bag
6-by-8-inch (15-by-20-cm)
  index card
magnifying lens

Draw a line about ½ inch (1.25 cm) from the short end of the smaller index card.

 Cut along the line to make a paper strip.

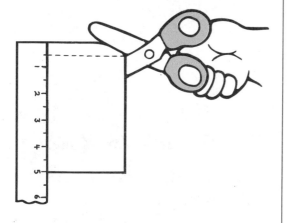

ADULT STEP Cut a 1-inch (2.5-cm) piece from the end of the craft stem. Push the piece of craft stem through the 3 marsh-

mallows so they are joined end to end to form the body of an insect.

Glue the center marshmallow to the middle of the paper strip as shown. Allow the glue to dry. This will take about 5 to 10 minutes.

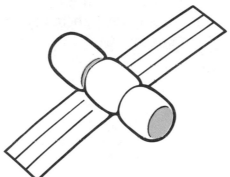

ADULT STEP Draw two lines on each side of the paper from the outer end toward the

marshmallow, dividing each side into three equal parts.

 Cut along the lines.

Bend the paper strips to form six legs.

Use the pen to draw two eyes on one of the end marshmallows. This marshmallow will be the insect's head.

ADULT STEP Break off about ½ inch (1.25 cm) from both ends of the toothpick. Discard the center of the toothpick.

Insert the pointed ends of the toothpick pieces into the head to make two antennae.

Set the insect on a table. Push the remaining, long piece of craft stem into the hind end of the insect. Have your friend hold the craft stem and make the insect slowly move around.

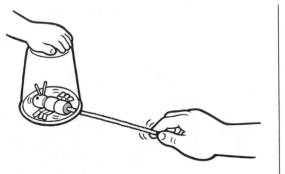

 Catch the insect by quickly, but gently, turning the plastic cup over the insect. This cup will be called the catching cup. Be careful not to "injure" the insect.

 Carefully slide the larger index card under the cup and the insect without giving the insect enough room to "sneak out."

Have your friend hold the insect in place with the catching cup while you pull out the craft stem.

 Use the magnifying lens to study your insect.

So Now We Know

You can catch real insects the same way that you caught your pretend insect. Using the catching cup and a magnifying lens, you can study insects up close without touching them. When you are done, just pick up the cup and let the insect walk or fly away.

More Fun Things to Know and Do

To study an insect more closely, you can move it to a plastic bag. Here's how to move an insect from the catching cup to a holding bag:

- **ADULT STEP** Use the pencil to make five or six small airholes through the plastic bag near the top so the insect from the original experiment has air to "breathe." This bag will

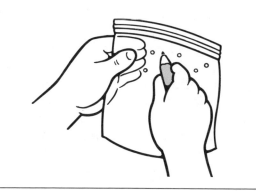

be called the holding bag.

- Hold the bag open while your friend dumps the insect from the collecting cup into the holding bag.

- Lay the index card on a table near a window or lamp.

- Place the holding bag with the insect on the card.

- Hold the insect stationary by gently pressing the bag next to its body. Then, use the magnifying lens to study the insect. Be careful not to squeeze the insect and "hurt" it.

Now you are ready to catch a real insect. Remember not to leave a live insect in the holding bag too long. After about 30 minutes, return the insect to where you found it. *CAUTION: Never touch an insect unless you know that it will not harm you.*

Sweeper

I wonder . . . How can I catch a flying insect?

Let's find out!

Round Up These Things

wire clothes hanger
masking tape
scissors
13-gallon (52-liter) tall
  plastic kitchen garbage
  bag with straight edges
pencil

Later You'll Need

insect net made in original
  experiment
large bowl of popped popcorn
pencil
1-gallon (4-liter) resealable
  plastic bag
*CAUTION: Never place a plastic
bag over your head or anyone
else's. The bag could prevent
you from breathing.*

1 **ADULT STEP** Shape the clothes hanger into a hoop and bend the hook closed.

2 Tape the hook closed to form a handle as shown.

3 **ADULT STEP** Cut diagonally across the tall kitchen garbage bag as shown. Keep the half with the open end and discard the rest of the bag.

4 Fold up about 1 inch (2.5 cm) of the cut edge of the plastic and tape it to make a plastic net.

5 **ADULT STEP** Use the pencil to punch 20 to 30 small airholes through the plastic near the closed end of the net.

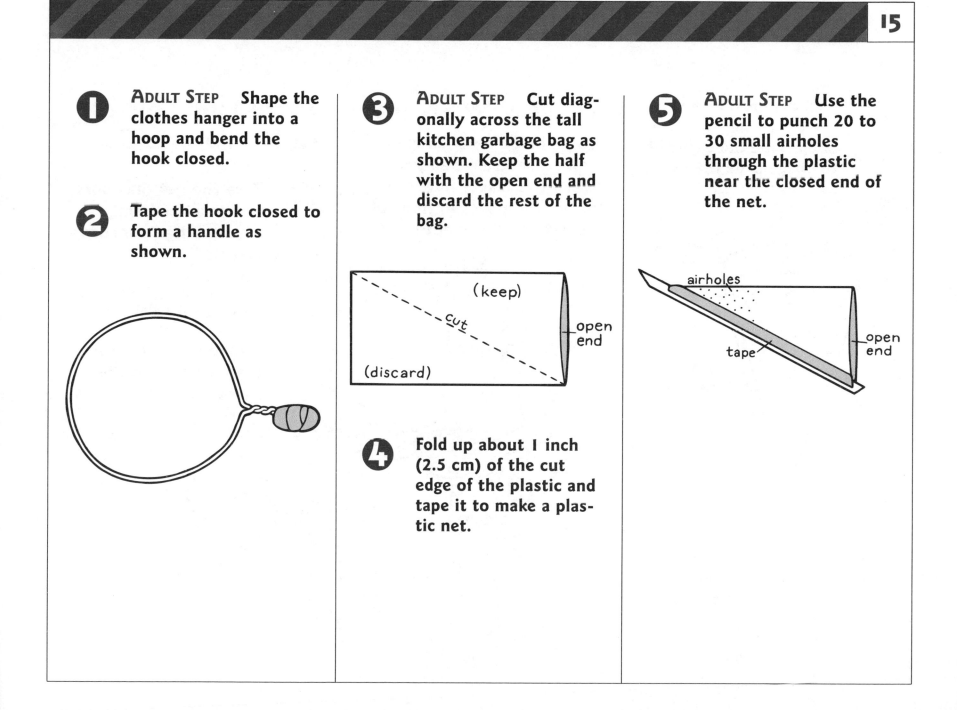

6 Fold the open end of the plastic net over the hoop. Tape the edges of the bag inside the net as shown.

tape

taped edge

7 Holding the handle, turn the net sideways and sweep its open end through the air. The plastic bag fills with air.

So Now We Know

You've made a net to catch flying insects. When you sweep the insect net through the air, an insect in front of the net can be swept inside.

More Fun Things to Know and Do

1 Take the net outdoors and practice using it by catching "popcorn insects."

- **ADULT STEP** Throw the popcorn into the air.

- Sweep the net through the air to catch the flying popcorn insects.

Once you have caught your popcorn insects, remove them from the net without touching them with your hands. Here's how:

- ADULT STEP Use the pencil to make 5 or 6 airholes in the 1-gallon (4-liter) plastic bag near the top. This bag will be called the holding bag.

- Squeeze the net closed near the hoop to keep the insects from escaping.

- ADULT STEP Hold the holding bag open.

- Holding the net over the bag, push the net through the hoop and into the bag. Turn the net inside out as you go, until you see the insect drop into the bag.

- Remove the net from the bag.

- ADULT STEP Seal the bag as soon as the net is removed.

Now that you have practiced using your net, catch a real flying insect. You can do this by sweeping the net through the air where bugs are flying, or across the top of grass or bushes where flying bugs might be resting. (See the next experiment for information on removing a butterfly from the net.) Remember, after about 30 minutes, release the bugs from the holding bag and return them to where you found them. *CAUTION: Do not touch a bug unless you know that it is harmless. Do not catch bees or wasps.*

Butterfly House

I wonder . . . How can I keep butterflies?

Let's find out!

Round Up These Things

scissors
ruler
18 inches (45 cm) of ⅛-inch (0.3-cm)-wide ribbon
3-by-6-foot (0.9-by-1.8-m) piece of netting (available at fabric stores)
12-inch (30-cm)-diameter corrugated cardboard disk
small branch

Later You'll Need

butterfly house made in original experiment
insect net from the experiment "Sweeper"
1-quart (1-liter) wide-mouthed plastic jar and lid with 2 to 4 airholes
magnifying lens
field guide to butterflies
1 tablespoon (15 ml) sugar
1 cup (150 ml) tap water
small butter dish
cotton balls

1 Cut a 12-inch (30-cm) and a 6-inch (15-cm) piece from the ribbon.

2 Fold the netting in half twice, putting the long sides together.

3 Bunch each short end of the netting together and tie each end closed with one of the pieces of ribbon.

4 Make a loop out of the long ribbon piece by tying its ends together.

5 ADULT STEP   Hang the netting by the loop.

6 Open the overlapped edges of the netting and place the cardboard disk inside on the bottom end. This will be your butterfly house.

7 Place a small branch inside the house for butterflies to rest on.

8 Close the edges of the netting again so that they are straight and overlap as much as possible.

So Now We Know

You have made a temporary home for butterflies. It lets in light and air and is tall enough for butterflies to fly around. When the butterfly house is hanging straight, the netting overlaps and butterflies can't get out. The branch provides a nice resting place for butterflies.

More Fun Things to Know and Do

Now that you have made your butterfly house, you will want to catch butterflies to put in it. The key thing to remember when catching butterflies is that they usually fly upward. Make an insect net and catch a butterfly using the instructions in the experiment "Sweeper." Butterflies are very fragile. Here is a way to get them out of the net without hurting them:

- Catch a butterfly in the net.

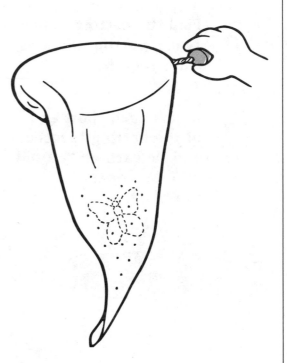

- Flip the hoop of the net over so that it's pointing toward the ground. The net will hang over one side of the hoop, closing the net.

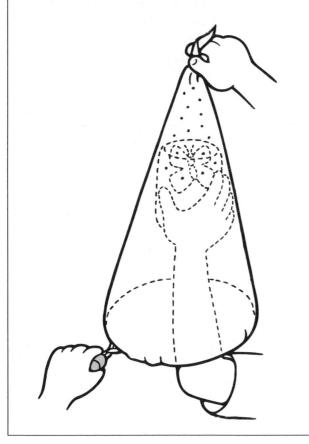

- **ADULT STEP** Move the open end of the jar into the net.

- Slowly lift the end of the net up. The butterfly will fly to the top of the net.

- **ADULT STEP** Move the jar around the butterfly, then turn the jar upside down so the butterfly will fly up into the jar. Slip the lid into the net and close the jar.

- Use the magnifying lens to make a close-up study of the butterfly in the jar. Use the field guide to identify the butterfly.

- Move the butterfly into the butterfly house by setting the jar right side up in the house. Open the lid and the butterfly will fly up and out of the jar.

- Feed the butterfly with homemade nectar by mixing together the sugar and water. Fill the dish with cotton balls and moisten them with the nectar. Place the dish inside the house. Remember, you only want to keep butterflies for 1 or 2 days, then release them so they can lay eggs to make more beautiful butterflies.

Bug House

Round Up These Things

2 cups (500 ml) dry sand or soil
1-gallon (4-liter) wide-mouthed jar
empty toilet tissue tube
scissors
dishwashing sponge
lid from a small jar
tap water
2 or 3 twigs that will fit inside the jar
2 tablespoons (30 ml) dry cereal
slice of raw apple
5 to 6 crickets (caught or purchased from a pet store)
knee-high stocking

Later You'll Need

your crickets from original experiment

1 Pour the sand into the jar.

2 Put the tube in the jar for the crickets to have a place to hide.

3 ADULT STEP Cut a round piece of sponge that will fit inside the lid.

4 Moisten the sponge with water, set it in the lid, and place the lid inside the jar. The crickets will drink the water from the sponge, so be sure to keep it moist while you have your crickets.

5 Add the twigs to the jar. The crickets will climb on the twigs.

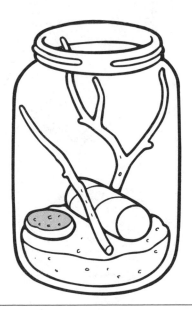

Drop the cereal and the apple slice into the jar. The crickets will eat this food, so add more when it is gone.

 Place your crickets in the jar and immediately cover the opening with the stocking. The stocking allows air in but keeps the crickets from escaping.

 Observe the crickets inside their house as often as possible for 1 to 2 weeks, then release them outdoors.

So Now We Know

You have made a house that crickets can live in. Watch your crickets as they eat, drink, and move around their home.

More Fun Things to Know and Do

Just for fun, you can name your crickets. To name a cricket, you need to know if it is a boy or a girl. This can be done by looking at its hind end. All crickets have two feelers on their hind end, but the female has a third tube that looks like a stinger. It's not a stinger, it's an egg-laying tube. Study the pictures of boy and girl crickets shown here to tell which of your crickets are boys and which are girls.

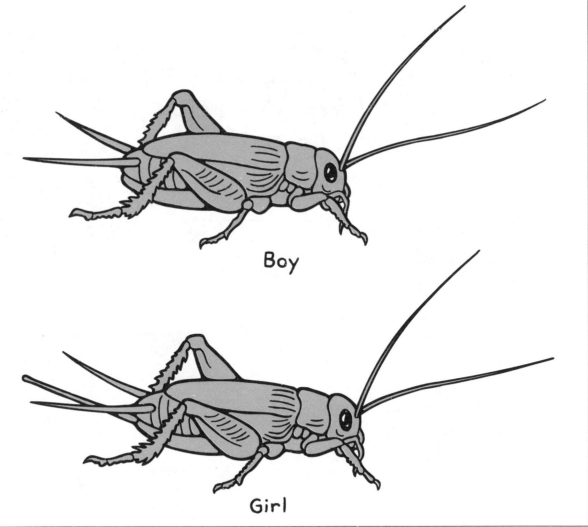

Boy

Girl

Tunnels

I wonder ... What's inside an anthill?

Let's find out!

Round Up These Things

sheet of 9-by-12-inch (22.5-by-30-cm) brown construction paper
pencil
ruler
scissors
sheet of typing paper
school glue

Later You'll Need

ant nest made in original experiment
pencil
dried prune
10 to 12 raisins
small bowl
large spoon
school glue
1 teaspoon (5 ml) rice
ant farm (optional)

1 On one of the long sides of the brown paper, draw a line with two hill shapes on it. Make the hills about 5 inches (12.5 cm) apart, 1 inch (2.5 cm) tall, and 2 inches (5 cm) wide.

2 Cut along the line and discard the cutaway edge of the paper.

3 Fold the typing paper in half, with the short sides together. Unfold the paper and cut along the fold line.

4 Draw five large ovals on one of the paper halves. The ovals do not have to be perfect or alike.

5 Cut out the ovals.

6 Glue the ovals to the brown paper as shown. These shapes represent the underground rooms in an ant nest.

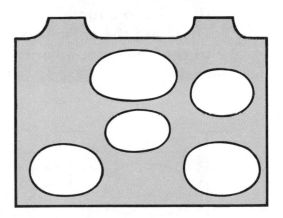

7 Fold the other half of the typing paper in half, with the short sides together, three times. Unfold the paper.

Cut along the fold lines to make 8 separate strips.

 Glue a strip of paper leading from each of the hills to a room. These are the entrances to the underground ant nest.

 Glue the remaining strips of paper between the rooms on the brown paper to represent tunnels. You may need to shorten the strips to fit between the rooms.

So Now We Know

In your house, you have rooms and connecting halls. An ant's house is called a nest. The houses of ants that live in the soil have rooms called chambers with connecting tunnels. As the ants dig the tunnels and rooms, they carry the dirt up to the surface and dump it, creating anthills.

More Fun Things to Know and Do

Ant chambers, just like the rooms in your house, are used for different things. Here's how to catch and place pretend ants in the different chambers of your ant nest:

• Label the chambers NURSERY, QUEEN, EGGS, FOOD, and TRASH as shown.

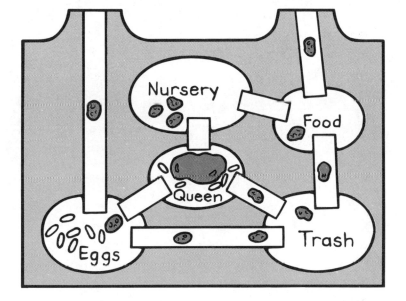

- Place the prune and the raisins in the bowl.

- Use the spoon to catch the queen ant, represented by the prune.

- Put the queen ant in the queen room and secure with glue.

- The raisins represent worker ants. Use the spoon to catch the worker ants one at a time. Glue them in place in different chambers and tunnels.

- The rice represents eggs. Glue some of the rice near the queen ant and the rest in the egg room.

- Compare the size of the queen and worker ants. Notice how much bigger the queen ant is.

2 For a close-up study of a colony, or city, of real ants in their nest, purchase an ant farm from a toy or science store. *CAUTION: Follow the instructions carefully in setting up your ant farm. Ants can get out if the farm is not properly closed. Do not do this activity if anyone who will be around the ant farm is allergic to ant stings.*

Changing

Around and Around

Let's find out!

Nursery

I wonder . . . Where do butterflies come from?

Round Up These Things

6-inch (15-cm) circle of blue construction paper
black marking pen
school glue
white paper plate
3-inch (7.5-cm) square of red construction paper
scissors
6-inch (15-cm) black chenille craft stem (available at craft stores) or pipe cleaner
3-by-4-inch (7.5-by-10-cm) piece of green construction paper
7 to 10 uncooked grains of rice
three ½-inch (1.25-cm) craft pom-poms (Iridescent ones work best.)
3-inch (7.5-cm) twig
12 inches (30 cm) of masking tape

Later You'll Need

6-inch (15-cm) circle of blue construction paper
black marking pen
school glue
white paper plate
pencil
2 crayons, green and brown
7 to 10 uncooked grains of rice

1 Fold the blue paper circle in half twice to divide the circle into four equal pie slices.

2 Unfold the paper and use the pen to draw a line along each fold line.

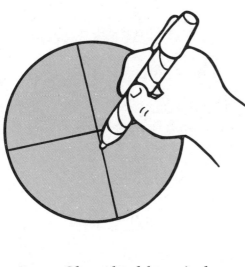

3 Glue the blue circle to the center of the paper plate.

4 Fold the red square in half and draw a wing shape as shown in the picture.

5 ADULT STEP Cut out the wings by cutting through both layers of paper.

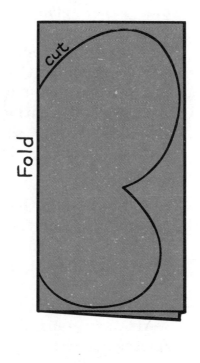

cut

Fold

6 Unfold the wings and use the pen to decorate the wings of the butterfly. Make the decorations on the left wings match those on the right wings.

7 Fold the craft stem in half and slip the center of the wings into the folded stem. The stem represents the butterfly's body. Twist the stem together to hold the body in place, then flare the ends of the stem outward to make antennae.

8 Glue the butterfly to one of the sections of the blue circle. This is the adult butterfly. Write ADULT on the plate.

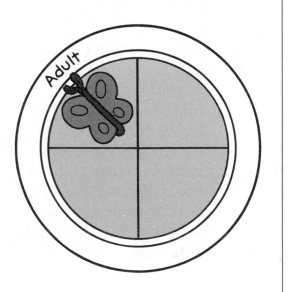

9 Cut 2 leaves from the green paper.

10 Glue one leaf to the section to the right of the butterfly. Glue the

rice grains to this leaf. The rice represents the eggs laid by the adult on the leaf. Write EGGS on the plate.

11 Tear a small piece out of the remaining leaf. Glue the leaf to the next section on the plate. Then, glue the pom-poms to the leaf. The pom-poms represent a caterpillar that has hatched from one of the eggs and is eating the leaf. Write CATERPILLAR on the plate.

12 Glue the twig to the last section. Roll the masking tape into a small tubelike shape and glue it next to the twig. The tape represents a chrysalis, the resting stage during

which a caterpillar changes into an adult. Write CHRYSALIS on the plate.

13 Draw arrows between the sections on the blue paper as shown.

14 Rotate the plate counterclockwise and see the changes a butterfly goes through.

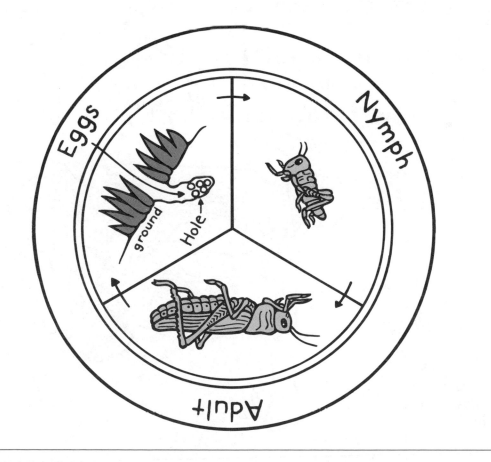

So Now We Know

The butterfly growth wheel shows an adult butterfly laying eggs. One of the eggs changes into a caterpillar and the caterpillar changes into a chrysalis. The chrysalis changes into another adult butterfly.

More Fun Things to Know and Do

An adult grasshopper lays her eggs in the ground. The eggs change into small grasshoppers called nymphs. The nymphs grow into adult grasshoppers. Using the procedure from the original experiment, make a grasshopper growth wheel by dividing the paper plate into three sections. Use the pencil to draw the different changes of the grasshopper as shown in the pictures here. Use the pen to label the changes. Color the grass green and the grasshopper brown. Glue the grains of rice to the egg section. Draw arrows between the sections as shown. Rotate the plate to see how a grasshopper grows up.

Break Out

1 Stand with your arms folded over your chest.

2 ADULT STEP   Wrap two layers of newspaper around the child's body, one layer around her chest and the other around her hips. Use tape to secure the papers together.

3 ADULT STEP   Hold the cookie to the child's mouth so she can take a bite.

4 Eat the bite of cookie, then pretend to grow by spreading your arms and pushing out on the paper. The paper around your chest will tear apart, but the paper around your hips will stay together.

5 Allow the paper to fall, then step out of the paper and leave it on the floor.

So Now We Know

Young grasshoppers eat and grow larger, but their outer covering, called an exoskeleton, does not grow. When a grasshopper's exoskeleton gets too tight, this covering splits and the grasshopper wiggles out just as you did when you broke out of the paper. The grasshopper has a new, larger exoskeleton underneath the old one.

More Fun Things to Know and Do

Some insects, such as butterflies, do not grow from smaller versions of themselves. Instead the butterfly grows by changing shape and form entirely. (See the experiment "Around and Around" for more on butterfly growth.) A special sac called a chrysalis forms around a caterpillar. The butterfly that emerges from the chrysalis is at its adult size. Here's a way to show these changes:

- Lay an open sleeping bag on the floor.

- Place the scarves inside the bag.

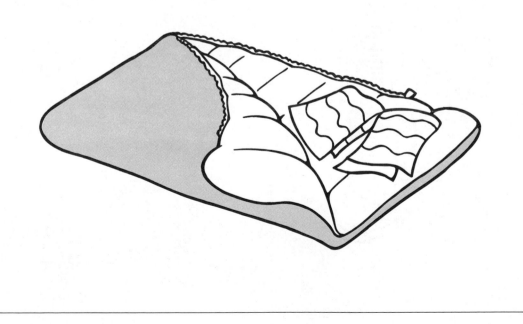

- Pretend to be a caterpillar and crawl inside the bag. Zip the bag closed over your body. The bag is your chrysalis.

- Inside the chrysalis, a caterpillar changes into a butterfly with wings.

- Find the scarves, and hold one in each hand. The scarves are your wings.

- During the change from a caterpillar to a butterfly, little or no movement inside the chrysalis is seen. Lie very still for a few seconds, then unzip the bag.

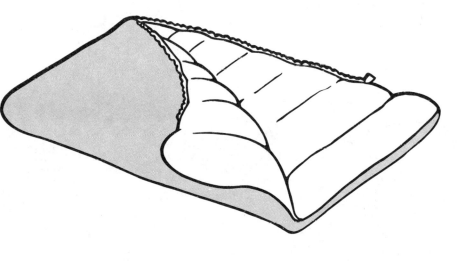

- At first, emerging butterflies are wet and need time to dry. Slowly crawl out, stand, and walk around very slowly with your arms and the scarf wings hanging by your body. Then, start flapping your wings as you pretend to be a flying butterfly.

Moving

Creepers

Let's find out!

I wonder ... How many legs do caterpillars have?

Round Up These Things

1-by-11-inch (2.5-by-27.5-cm)
 strip of typing paper
scissors
black marking pen
ruler
no. 10 crochet thread
4-ply knitting yarn
transparent tape

Later You'll Need

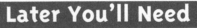

caterpillar made in original
 experiment

① Fold the paper in half four times, with the short ends together. Unfold the paper.

② Cut off and discard two sections of one end of the strip.

③ Refold the strip, making accordion folds along the length of the paper.

The 12 dots represent eyes, 6 on each side of the head.

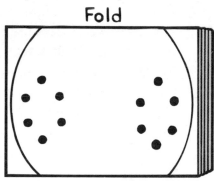

Fold

⑤ ADULT STEP   Cut along both curved lines drawn on the paper, cutting through all layers of the paper.

④ With the strip completely folded, draw two curved lines and 12 dots on one end section as shown. This section will be the caterpillar's head.

⑥ Stretch the paper out. Starting with the segment next to the head, number the body segments from 1 through 13.

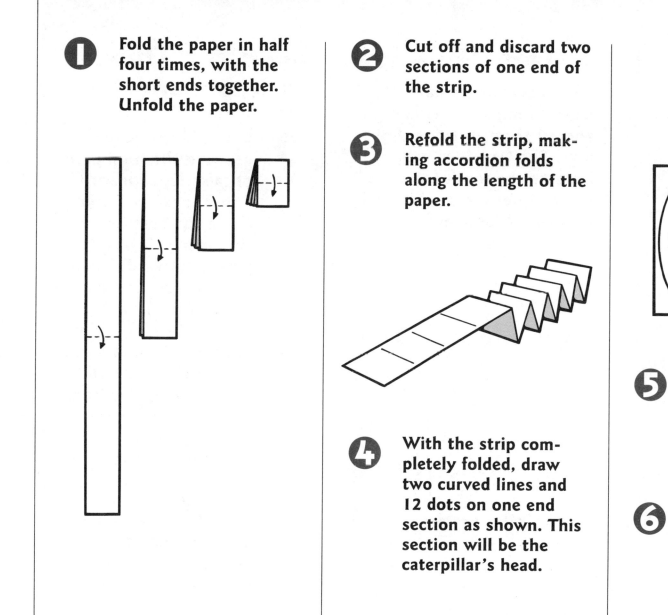

Cut three 2-inch (5-cm) pieces of crochet thread and five 1¼-inch (3-cm) pieces of yarn.

 Tape a thread across each of the first three body segments. These threads represent the true legs of the caterpillar.

9 Tape the yarn across segments 6, 7, 8, 9, and 13. The thick yarn represents false legs.

So Now We Know

Most caterpillars have 16 legs: 6 long, thin, true legs; and 10 shorter, fatter, false legs. The true legs will become the legs of the adult butterfly or moth. The false legs will disappear.

More Fun Things to Know and Do

1 Caterpillars move by drawing the hind pair of false legs forward. These legs then hold on to the surface as the next pair of legs moves forward. Each pair of legs moves forward, one after the other. The caterpillar's body moves in a wave-like motion. Use the paper caterpillar from the original experiment to show how a caterpillar moves.

- Refold your caterpillar and place it on a flat surface, such as a table.

- Hold the head segment in one hand and the hind segment in the other hand.

- Push the hind segment forward, moving the body segments closer together.

- Pull the head segment forward, moving the body segments farther apart. Your caterpillar shows how a real caterpillar moves.

② Catch a caterpillar using the instructions in the experiment "Trapper." Transfer the caterpillar to a 1-gallon (4-liter) jar that has a branch inside. Observe the movement of the caterpillar. If you wish to keep the caterpillar and watch it change into a moth or butterfly, put in the jar some of the plants the caterpillar was found eating and add more when they have been eaten. Remove the caterpillar and clean out the jar every 2 to 3 days. Use a field guide to caterpillars, such as *Peterson's First Guides to Caterpillars* by Amy Bartlett Wright (New York: Houghton Mifflin, 1993), to identify your caterpillar and find out how long it will take to make the change. See the experiment "Around and Around" for information on the different growth stages. *CAUTION: Unless you know the caterpillar is harmless, do not touch it or pick it up.*

Lifters

Round Up These Things

sheet of typing paper
2-by-1-by-½-inch (5-by-
  2.5-by-1.25-cm) block
  of modeling clay
6 round toothpicks

Later You'll Need

black marking pen
labels
2 friends

1 Place the paper on a table and set the clay on the paper.

2 Use one of the tooth-picks to make 6 dots in the clay.

3 Stick one toothpick into each marked dot on the clay. Make sure each toothpick sticks out the same amount from the clay. The clay represents a bug's body and the toothpicks represent its legs.

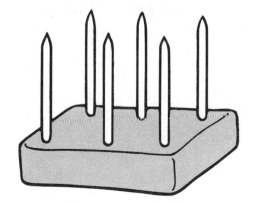

4 Turn the bug body over and stand it on the 6 toothpick legs. The body will not wobble if the toothpick legs are all the same length.

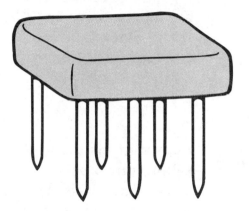

Take any 3 of the toothpick legs out of the clay body.

 Try to stand the bug body on its 3 toothpick legs. Be sure the legs are all the same length. If the block falls, put the legs back in and continue with the next step.

7 Repeat steps 5 and 6, taking out 3 other toothpicks. Keep trying different combinations until the body stands.

So Now We Know

Bugs with six legs balance on just three of their legs, if they are the right ones. The three legs that they must keep on the ground are the front and hind legs on one side, plus the middle leg on the opposite side. Then they can lift the other three legs to walk.

More Fun Things to Know and Do

As a bug walks, three legs support the weight of the body while the other three legs swing forward to a new position. To walk like a grasshopper, ant, or ladybug, try this:

- Form a line with 2 friends, one behind the other. Place your hands on each other's shoulders.

- ADULT STEP Write the numbers 1 through 6 on the labels, and place the labels on the children's shoes as shown.

Walk with your friends, lifting your feet as follows:

1. First lift and move forward feet 1, 2, and 3.

2. Next, lift and move forward feet 4, 5, and 6.

3. Repeat the steps several times.

Sticky Feet

1 Fold the paper strip in half twice, putting the short ends of the paper together.

2 Unfold the paper, then refold it accordion-style.

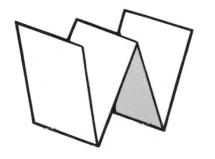

3 Fill the bowl about half full with water.

4 Stick your finger into the bowl of water and use your wet fingertip to moisten the outside end section of the paper strip. This section represents the end of the leg, or the "foot," of a bug.

5 ADULT STEP   Hold the saucer upright. Touch the wet foot to the saucer's underside. Release the paper. The paper leg sticks to the saucer.

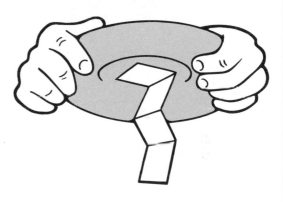

So Now We Know

Flies have moisture on their feet. Like the wet paper, the wet feet of a fly can stick to a ceiling and keep the fly from falling.

More Fun Things to Know and Do

You cannot walk on the ceiling, but you can see how the world would look if you could. Here's how:

- Stand holding the edge of the mirror under your chin as shown.

- ADULT STEP Guide the child as you walk through the house together.

- Look down into the mirror as you walk around. How does your house look upside down?

Water Walkers

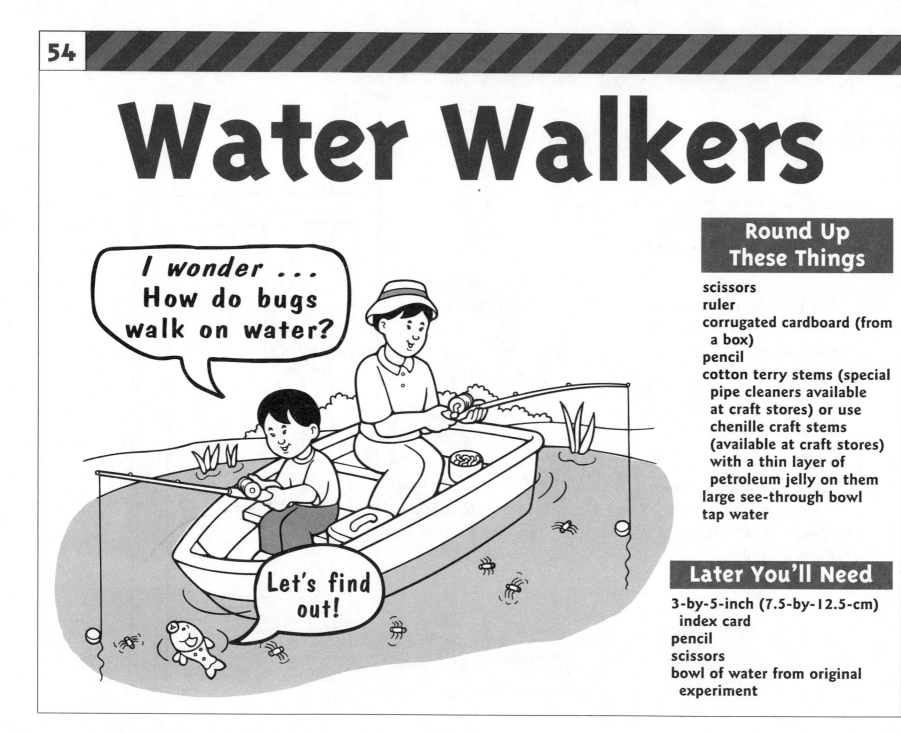

Round Up These Things

scissors
ruler
corrugated cardboard (from a box)
pencil
cotton terry stems (special pipe cleaners available at craft stores) or use chenille craft stems (available at craft stores) with a thin layer of petroleum jelly on them
large see-through bowl
tap water

Later You'll Need

3-by-5-inch (7.5-by-12.5-cm) index card
pencil
scissors
bowl of water from original experiment

① ADULT STEP Cut a 3-by-1-inch (7.5-by-2.5-cm) strip from the cardboard, cutting the 3-inch (7.5-cm) sides against the grooves. This strip will be the body of the bug. Shape the strip by cutting notches.

② Draw eyes at one end of the strip as shown.

③ ADULT STEP Cut three 3-inch (7.5-cm) pieces from the cotton terry stems.

④ Stick each piece of stem all the way through three grooves in the second section of the bug's body so that the same amount of stem sticks out on either side. Put one stem at each end of the section and one in the center. The stems will be the legs of the bug.

⑤ Bend each leg down where it meets the bug's body. Then, bend about ¼ inch (0.6 cm) of the end of each leg out to form a foot. Stand the bug on a table and adjust the bends in the legs so that each foot touches the table.

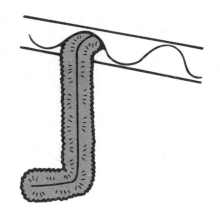

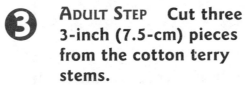

3 in. (7.5 cm)

1 in. (2.5 cm)

6 Fill the bowl three-fourths full with water.

7 Slowly lower the bug until its feet touch the surface of the water. Then release it. The bug will stand on the water's surface.

So Now We Know

Some lightweight bugs can walk on water because the surface of the water acts as if it has a thin skin on it. The bugs can stand and walk across this surface the same way your cardboard bug stayed on the surface of the water.

More Fun Things to Know and Do

Bugs come in many different shapes and sizes, but if they are lightweight enough the skinlike surface of the water will hold them up. Here's how to make another bug that will stand on water:

- Fold the index card in half with the long sides together.

- Use the pattern shown to draw a bug on the card.

- Use a pencil to divide the bug's body into three sections and to draw two eyes on its head.

- ADULT STEP Cut out the bug.

- Bend the end of the bug's paper legs to form feet.

- Stand the paper bug on the surface of the water in the bowl.

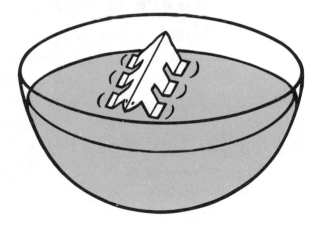

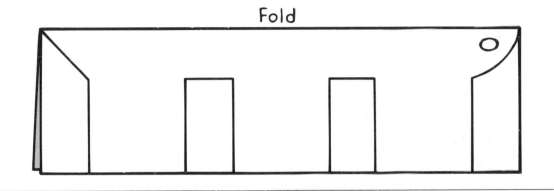

Fold

Speedy

I wonder ... Is there a dragon that can fly?

Let's find out!

Round Up These Things

3-by-9-inch (7.5-by-22.5-cm) piece of colorless transparent plastic (A report cover works well.)

black, fine-point, permanent marker

scissors

two 12-inch (30-cm) brown chenille craft stems (available at craft stores) or pipe cleaners

school glue

two 10-mm wiggle eyes (available at craft stores)

Later You'll Need

the same materials
but
substitute 2 light blue craft stems for 2 brown ones

1. Lay the piece of plastic over the dragonfly wing pattern shown here.

2. Use the marker to trace the shape and line patterns of the wings.

3. **ADULT STEP** Cut out the wings without cutting them apart.

4. Twist the ends of one craft stem together to form 2 short antennae, then twist the stem a short distance away from the antennae to form a loop for the head. This will leave a loop for the body.

5. **ADULT STEP** Cut the second craft stem in half. Cut one of the halves into 3 equal parts. Keep the longer piece for later.

6. Hold the 3 pieces of craft stem together and twist them at the center to form the legs.

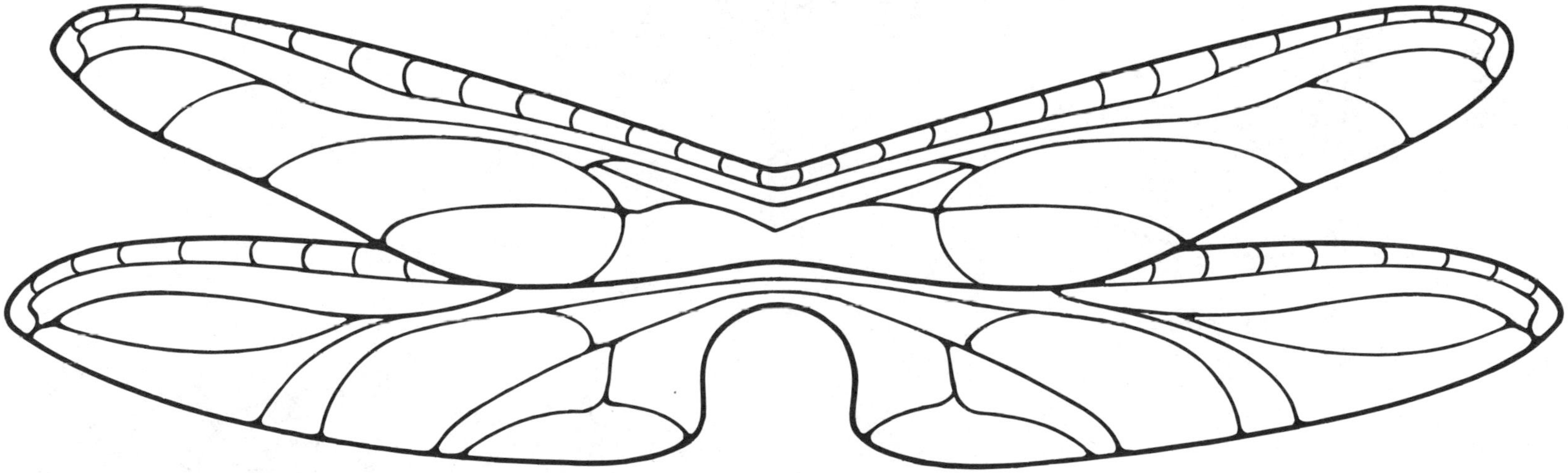

Dragonfly Wing Pattern

7 Slip the legs and wings through the body loop, close to the head loop, then twist the body loop around the legs and wings till they are held tight. This part of the dragonfly is called the thorax. Twist the rest of the body loop together to form the abdomen as shown.

8 Wrap the half piece of craft stem from step 5 around the abdomen to make it fatter.

9 Glue the eyes to the head.

So Now We Know

You have made a model of a dragonfly. Dragons are fairy-tale animals. But there is an insect called a dragonfly. These insects have four big wings, and the hind wings are a little larger than the front wings. Dragonflies are very speedy and have been known to fly 50 to 60 miles per hour (80 to 96 kmph).

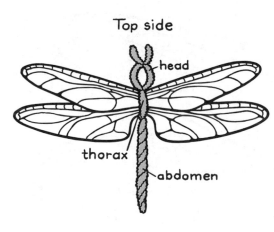

Top side

head

thorax

abdomen

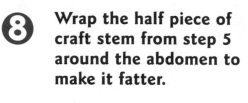

Underside

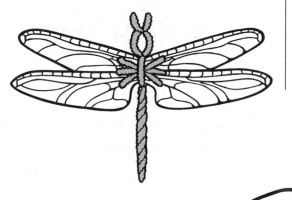

More Fun Things to Know and Do

1 Damselflies look very much like dragonflies, except damselflies' front and hind wings are about the same size and narrow near their bodies. Their abdomens are smaller. Make a model of a damselfly by following the steps for making a dragonfly, except:

- Make the wings by using the damselfly wing pattern.

- Do not twist the half piece of craft stem around the abdomen.

2 When these insects are flying, it is hard to compare their wing and body sizes. It is easier to tell a damselfly from a dragonfly by the way they hold their wings when resting. The dragonfly holds its wings straight out, but the damselfly holds its wings together above its back. Watch for these insects and identify them when you observe them at rest.

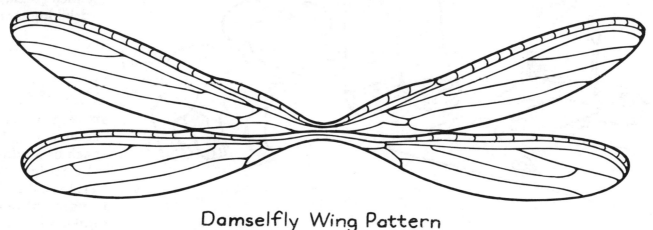

Damselfly Wing Pattern

Flutter

Round Up These Things

ruler
transparent tape
1-by-8½-inch (2.5-by-21.25-cm) strip of paper
¼-inch (6-cm)-diameter drinking straw

Later You'll Need

six ¾-inch (1.9-cm) round color-coding labels, two each of 3 different colors
1-by-8½-inch (2.5-by-21.25-cm) strip of paper
transparent tape
drinking straw

1 Place half of a 1-inch (2.5-cm) piece of tape over one end of the paper. The other half of the tape will extend past the paper. The paper represents an insect wing.

 2 Lay the paper wing on a table with the sticky side of the tape face up.

3 Place the straw over the tape and paper wing so that about ¼ inch (0.63 cm) of the straw is on the paper as shown.

4 Wrap the tape around the straw.

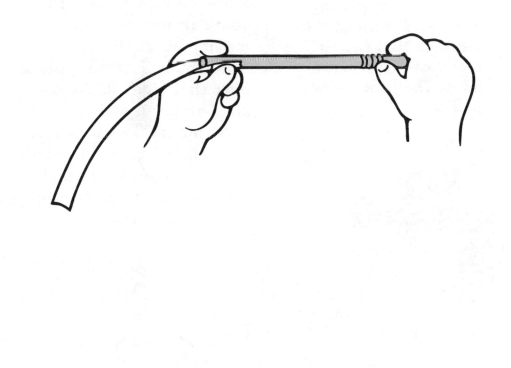

Place the straw in your mouth, with the straw above the paper wing. Blow hard through the straw so that the air blows over the paper wing. The paper wing lifts up.

So Now We Know

Some air moves fast, and some air moves slow. Slow-moving air pushes more against the surface it moves over than does fast-moving air. The paper strip of the wing model, like an insect wing, lifted because the air above it moved faster, allowing the slower air underneath it to push it up.

More Fun Things to Know and Do

Butterflies have tiny colored scales on their wings. Touching a butterfly's wings doesn't kill the insect, but it can remove or bend the scales. When scales are missing or bent, the butterfly has difficulty flying. Here's a way you can show this:

- Place a row of 2 labels side by side across the paper strip about 2 inches (5 cm) from one short end. The first label goes next to the long edge of the paper strip. The second label will stick out from the opposite edge.

- Add 2 more rows of colored labels across the paper. Start each row on the opposite edge of the paper, and overlap the labels in the previous row, as shown.

- Following steps 1 through 4 of the original experiment, attach a straw to your paper butterfly wing.

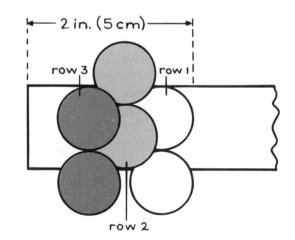

- Cut off the parts of the labels that stick out from the edges of the paper. This will be your butterfly wing.

- Blow hard through the straw over the paper wing so it lifts.

- Bend up 1 or 2 of the labels near the straw and again blow hard through the straw. The bent labels stop the flow of air and the wing does not lift.

Springy

**Round Up
These Things**

ruler
file folder
pencil
scissors
school glue
black marking pen

Later You'll Need

flea hopper made in original
 experiment
materials to make more flea
 hoppers
masking tape
small Post-it notes
black marking pen

1 Lay the ruler across the widest part of the closed file folder.

2 Use the pencil to draw two lines on the folder, one on each side of the ruler.

3 ADULT STEP Cut along both lines on the folder, cutting through both layers of the folder. Keep the 2 strips.

4 Lay the ends of the strips at right angles, as shown, and glue the corners together. Label the strips A and B.

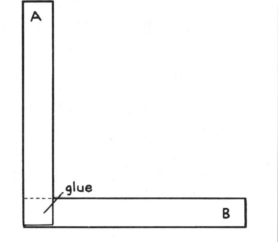

5 When the glue dries, fold strip B (the bottom strip) over strip A (the top strip).

6 Repeat step 5, folding the bottom strip over the top strip, until the strips are completely folded. Glue the ends together. This paper spring will be your flea hopper.

7 Stand the flea hopper on a flat surface, such as the floor. Push the folds of the flea hopper together with one finger, then quickly slide your finger off and watch the flea hopper jump up.

So Now We Know

Before a flea jumps, the springlike material in its hind legs is pushed together, like the spring in your flea hopper. When the flea's legs stretch out again, the "springs" push the legs forward and the flea jumps through the air.

More Fun Things to Know and Do

If the size of the body is considered, fleas would win the gold medal in any Olympic jumping contest. Some fleas can jump 12 inches (30 cm) or more. This is almost 200 times the flea's body length. If you could jump like a flea, you could hop over a 50-story building! Have a "flea Olympics" with the flea hopper you made in the original experiment.

- Invite friends to make flea hoppers. Experiment by using different widths and lengths of paper strips for each flea hopper.

- Test one hopper at a time. Place it on a starting line made with a piece of masking tape on the floor. Mark where the hopper first lands, using a Post-it note with the name of the person testing the hopper.

Communicating

Dancers

I wonder . . . Do bees dance?

Let's find out!

Round Up These Things

7 sheets of white copy paper
7 sheets of colored copy paper (any color)
pencil
scissors
black marking pen
masking tape
candy bar
ruler

Later You'll Need

dance pattern made in original experiment
candy bar

1 Fold one white and one colored sheet of paper in half (short ends together).

2 Unfold the white paper and make an outline of your right shoe on each side of the fold line on the paper.

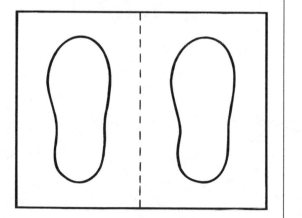

3 Repeat step 2, using the colored paper and your left shoe.

4 ADULT STEP Stack the rest of the white papers and put the sheet with the shoe outlines on top. Cut out the 2 outlines, cutting through all seven layers.

5 ADULT STEP Repeat step 4, using the colored papers.

6 Use the pen to number 8 of the white shoe cutouts with odd numbers from 1 through 15. Number the 6 remaining white shoe cutouts with odd numbers from 5 through 15.

7 Number 8 of the colored shoe cutouts with even numbers from 2 through 16. Number the 6 remaining colored shoe cutouts with even numbers from 6 through 16.

8 Lay the shoe cutouts on the floor in the pattern shown here. Use the tape to secure the cutouts to the floor. This is the pattern of a bee's dance.

9 Place the candy bar in its wrapper on the floor in line with the center line of the dance pattern and as far as possible from the pattern.

10 Stand with your right foot on the white number 1 cutout and your left foot on the colored number 2 cutout. You will be facing in the direction of the candy bar.

11 Walk forward, placing your feet on cutouts 3

and 4. Then, step on cutout 5 on the left side of the pattern and walk around the left side and through the center. When you reach cutout 4 again, step on cutout 5 on the right and walk around the right side. Follow the path several times. You are doing a bee dance called the waggle dance.

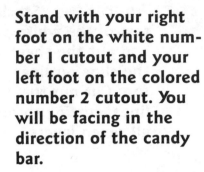

So Now We Know

Bees tell each other where faraway food is by doing a waggle dance. (By the way, bees eat nectar from flowers, not candy bars! And all of the bees that collect nectar are female.) The bee first flies in a straight line that points toward the food. She flies in a circle around one side of the line to get back to her starting place, then retraces the straight line and flies in a circle around the other side. She moves from one side to the other, making a pattern that looks like the number 8.

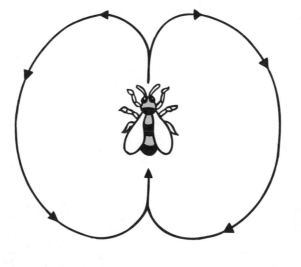

More Fun Things to Know and Do

The straight line through the bee's dance pattern indicates the direction of the food, but it's the movement of the bee's body along the straight line that indicates how far away the food is. To tell distance, she waggles her head and body, moving them quickly from side to side. The faster she waggles, the farther away the food is. Thus, the dance is called the waggle dance. Move through the dance pattern on the floor again, this time waggling your body as you move along the straight line. Take turns doing the waggle dance with a friend. Repeat, moving the candy bar about 1 foot (30 cm) closer to the pattern and waggling your body slower.

Flashers

I wonder . . . Why do fireflies light up?

Let's find out!

Round Up These Things

empty paper towel tube
1-ounce (30-ml) light stick (available where camping supplies are sold)

Later You'll Need

scissors
10-by-12-inch (25-by-30-cm) sheet of brown construction paper
20-ounce (600-ml) clear straight-sided plastic bottle with lid
transparent tape
school glue
two 7-mm wiggle eyes (available at craft stores)
12-inch (30-cm) yellow chenille craft stem (available at craft stores) or pipe cleaner
pencil
activated light stick from original experiment
CAUTION: Do not break the light stick open, because it has glass inside. The contents of light sticks are nontoxic, so the light stick may be disposed of by throwing it in the trash.

1 Stand the paper tube on a chair. Close one eye and look inside the tube with the open eye. It is dark inside the tube.

2 Remove the light stick from the package and drop it into the tube. Again, look inside the tube as before. It is still dark inside the tube.

3 ADULT STEP Remove the light stick from the tube, and activate the light by following the instructions on the package.

4 Again, drop the light stick into the tube and look inside the tube. The light stick gives off light and the inside of the tube glows.

So Now We Know

When the light stick was activated, a glass tube inside it broke and chemicals mixed together. The mixing of the chemicals produced light. A firefly, like the light stick, gives off light when chemicals in its abdomen mix together.

More Fun Things to Know and Do

In most kinds of fireflies, the female is wingless or has very short wings. Because of this, the male does most of the flying and the female usually remains on the ground or on low plants. They find each other by flashing their lights. Here's how to make a male firefly model:

- Fold the brown paper in half lengthwise. Cut the paper in half along the fold line.

- Wrap half the paper around the bottle and secure with tape.

- Press the top of the paper around the neck of the bottle and secure with

tape. This paper-covered area will be the firefly's thorax.

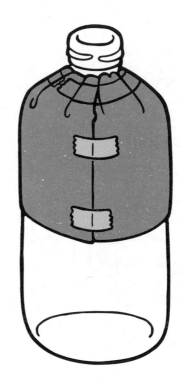

- Screw the lid on the bottle and glue the eyes to the top of the lid.

- Wrap the craft stem around the neck of the bottle and bend the ends to form antennae above the eyes.

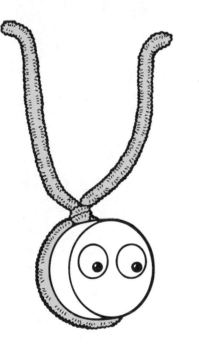

- Fold the remaining half of the brown paper in half twice, making a 3-by-5-inch (7.5-by-12.5-cm) rectangle.

- Draw the wing and leg patterns on the top layer of the folded paper.

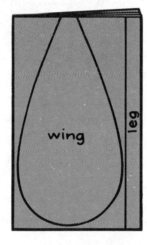

wing   leg

- **ADULT STEP** Cut out the drawings, cutting through all four layers. Discard one of the leg cutouts.

- Arrange the 4 wings in a fanlike pattern with the front wings overlapping the hind wings. Glue

them to the upper side of the thorax.

- Glue 3 of the leg cutouts by their centers to the underside of the thorax. Bend the ends, forming 6 legs.

- Unscrew the lid, place the activated light stick inside the bottle, then replace the lid. You now have a model of a male firefly that glows with a cool light.

Eating

Munchers

Round Up These Things

¼-by-6-inch (0.63-by-15-cm) strip of paper
ruler
transparent tape
pliers
hand soap
tap water
paper towel
cookie
mirror

Later You'll Need

another cookie
glass of milk

Bend up 2½ inches (6.25 cm) of each end of the paper strip.

 Bend out ½ inch (1.25 cm) of each end of the paper strip.

 Tape the center of the paper strip to the pliers as shown. The pliers represent a bug and the paper strip represents the bug's antennae.

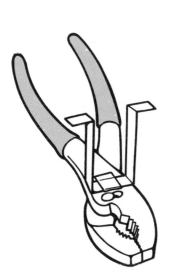

 Open the jaws of the pliers and use your fingertip to feel the parts that would touch if the jaws were closed. The jaws of the pliers feel rough, like the jaws of some insects.

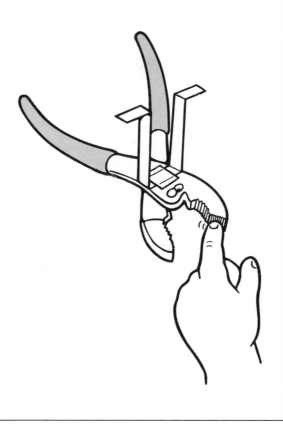

 Wash and dry your hands.

Open your mouth and feel the parts of your back teeth that touch when your mouth is closed. The surfaces of your teeth feel rough.

7 Hold the handles of the pliers, one in each hand, and open and close the jaws as shown. The jaws of the pliers open and close from side to side like the jaws of some insects.

8 Take a bite out of the cookie and eat it. Watch the motion of your jaws in the mirror as you chew. Your lower jaw moves up and down as your teeth crush the cookie.

chomp! chomp!

So Now We Know

Bugs don't have teeth like yours, but some, such as grasshoppers, have rough ridges on their jaws that are used for cutting and chewing food. These jaws open and close sideways, like the pliers, instead of up and down like your jaws.

More Fun Things to Know and Do

Not all insects have "chewing" mouthparts. Some, such as houseflies, have soaking and sucking mouthparts. The sucking mouthpart is a tube called a proboscis, which has a spongelike tip. A fly soaks up liquids with the spongy tip of its proboscis, then sucks the liquids into its body. Here's how you can eat like a fly:

- Dip the edge of a cookie into a glass of milk.

- Place the wet end of the cookie in your mouth and suck the milk from it.

Sippers

I wonder ...
How do butterflies drink?

Let's find out!

Round Up These Things

3-ounce (90-ml) paper cup
sheet of colored construction paper
  (any flower color)
pencil
scissors
¼ teaspoon (1.25 ml) sugar
1 tablespoon (15 ml) tap water
spoon
drinking straw

Later You'll Need

party blower

1 Turn the cup upside down and set it in the center of the paper.

2 With the pencil, trace around the outside of the cup.

3 Remove the cup and draw 6 large flower petals around the circle on the paper. Add a seam line as shown.

4 ADULT STEP Cut out the flower. Cut along the seam line, and then cut out the inner circle of the flower.

5 Slip the paper cup through the hole in the flower.

6 Put the sugar and the water in the cup. Stir.

cut out

seam

7 Stand the straw in the cup and sip the water.

So Now We Know

Inside flowers there is a sweet liquid called nectar. A butterfly drinks the nectar in flowers with a proboscis, a long feeding tube. You used a straw to drink the "nectar" in your paper flower.

More Fun Things to Know and Do

When a butterfly is not feeding, its proboscis is coiled up. The proboscis uncoils like a party blower when the butterfly wants to drink nectar from inside a flower. Use an upside-down party blower to show how a butterfly's proboscis coils and uncoils.

Camouflaging

Hide-and-Seek

Let's find out!

I wonder ... Why are walkingsticks hard to find?

Round Up These Things

craft stick
5 tablespoons (75 ml) plaster of paris
2 tablespoons (30 ml) tap water
3-ounce (90-ml) paper cup
three 12-inch (30-cm) brown chenille craft stems (available at craft stores) or pipe cleaners
scissors
ruler

Later You'll Need

scissors
ruler
20 or more chenille craft stems in different colors
100 feet (30 m) of string
friend

Use the craft stick to mix the plaster of paris and the water in the paper cup. Discard the craft stick. *NOTE: Do not wash plaster down the drain. It can clog the drain.*

2 Bend one of the craft stems into a V shape. Push the bent end into the wet plaster. This craft stem will be the two main stems of a bush. Allow the plaster to harden before starting the next step. This takes about 2 hours.

3 ADULT STEP Cut the second craft stem into 4 equal parts.

4 Twist the pieces around the stems in the plaster as shown to form branches on the bush.

5 ADULT STEP Cut a 4-inch (10-cm) piece from the third craft stem. Cut the remaining piece into four 2-inch (5-cm) pieces.

6 Twist the 4 shorter craft stem pieces around the longer piece to form 6 legs and 2 antennae as shown. You have made a walking-stick, an insect that looks like a small stick with branches.

7 Place the walkingstick on the bush. It is hard to tell the walkingstick from the branches.

So Now We Know

The shape and the color of a walkingstick are so much like the twigs of a tree that it is hard to see a walkingstick in a tree. This protects the walkingstick from animals that would eat it.

More Fun Things to Know and Do

Many insects blend in with their surroundings because they are the same shape and/or color as their surroundings. Here's an insect hide-and-seek game to play:

- Use the craft stems to make 20 or more insects. The insects should have different shapes and be different colors.

- Lay a string on the ground outdoors to mark a continuous trail about 100 feet (30 m) long. The trail should have grass, trees, and flowers, if possible.

- Without anyone watching, place the insects along one side of the string trail. The insects should be hard to see, but still visible.

- Take a friend outdoors and point out the side of the trail where the insects have been placed. Give your friend one minute to walk along the string trail and find as many insects as possible.

- If you have a number of friends who want to search, make more insects, have several trails, and search in teams.

Top and Bottom

I wonder ... Why is the top of a butterfly's wings a different color than the bottom?

Let's find out!

RED

BLUE

Round Up These Things

scissors
ruler
9-by-12-inch (22.5-by-30-cm) sheet of brown construction paper
black marking pen
2 cotton swabs
craft paints, red and yellow

Later You'll Need

doll pin (wooden clip clothespin, available at craft stores)
two 12-inch (30-cm) black chenille craft stems (available at craft stores) or pipe cleaners

1 Draw a line across one end of the paper, 4 inches (10 cm) from the end. Cut across the line, keeping the 4-inch (10-cm)-wide strip for the next step. Keep the larger piece of paper for step 10.

2 Fold the strip of paper in half, short ends together.

3 Draw the outline of a pair of butterfly wings on the paper as shown. Make the straight section along the fold about 1 inch (2.5 cm) long.

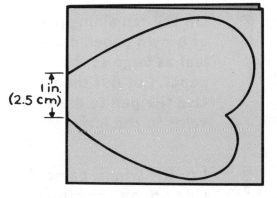

1 in. (2.5 cm)

4 **ADULT STEP** Cut out the wing drawing, cutting through both layers of paper. Do not cut the wings apart on the fold line.

5 Unfold the wings, then use the pen to draw a curved line between the top and bottom wings as shown. Draw the line on both the front and the back of the wings.

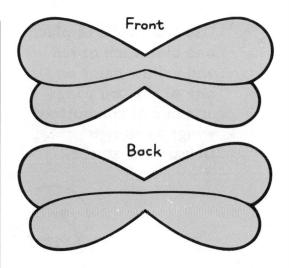

Front

Back

6 On the front of the wings, use the pen to draw a design that is the same on both the right and left wings as shown.

7 Use the swabs to place one blob each of red and yellow paint on one of the top wings and one of the bottom wings as shown. Discard the swabs.

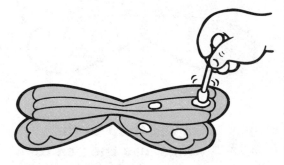

8 While the paint is still wet, refold the wings, painted sides together. Use your fingers to press the paint blobs and spread the wet paint as much as possible.

9 Unfold the wings and allow the paint to dry.

10 On the remaining piece of brown paper, draw a leaf as large as the paper. Cut out the leaf. Use the pen to draw veins in the leaf.

11 Lay the wings, painted side up, on the brown leaf. The colored wings are very easy to see.

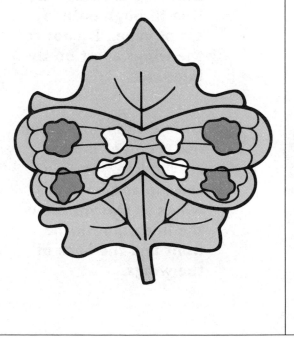

12 Fold the wings so that the colored sides are close together. Stand the folded wings on the leaf. The color of the underside of the wings and the color of the leaf blend together.

So Now We Know

On the top side, a butterfly's wings are very colorful. These colors are seen when the butterfly has its wings spread open as it flies. On the underside, the butterfly's wings are generally a dull color. When the butterfly rests, it holds its wings together, showing the underside. The dull color blends in with things that the butterfly stands on, making it hard to see the butterfly.

More Fun Things to Know and Do

Here's how to make a butterfly using the wings from the original experiment:

- Use the pen to draw 2 large eyes on the rounded end of the doll pin.

- ADULT STEP   Cut the 2 craft stems in half.

- Twist the pieces of craft stem around the doll pin to form 6 legs and 2 antennae as shown.

- Fold the wings, colored sides together. Run a bead of glue along both sides of the folded edge.

- Slip the folded edge in the slit of the doll pin. Open the wings.

The colored side of the wings should be face up, with the larger wing pair toward the head.

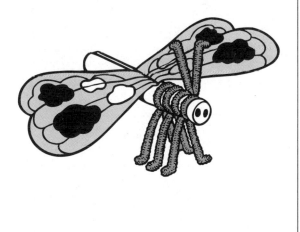

Spinning

Over the Edge

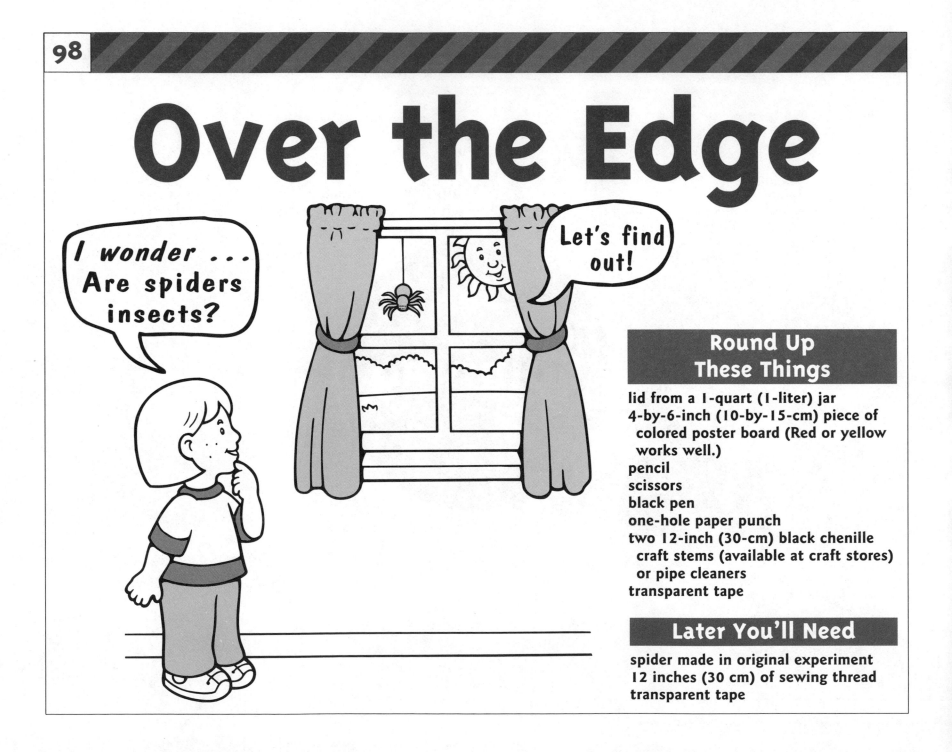

I wonder ... Are spiders insects?

Let's find out!

Round Up These Things

lid from a 1-quart (1-liter) jar
4-by-6-inch (10-by-15-cm) piece of
  colored poster board (Red or yellow
  works well.)
pencil
scissors
black pen
one-hole paper punch
two 12-inch (30-cm) black chenille
  craft stems (available at craft stores)
  or pipe cleaners
transparent tape

Later You'll Need

spider made in original experiment
12 inches (30 cm) of sewing thread
transparent tape

① Lay the lid near one end of the poster board.

② Use the pencil to trace around the lid.

③ Move the lid up so that it slightly overlaps the first tracing, then again trace around the lid.

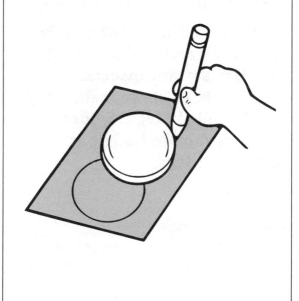

④ Draw part of a circle at the top of the second circle, following the picture shown. You have drawn the outline of a spider. Mark UNDERSIDE on the spider as shown.

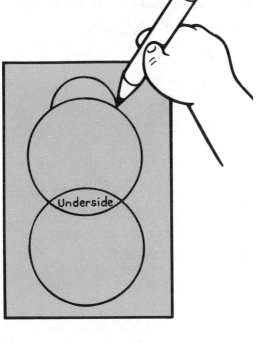

Underside

⑤ ADULT STEP   Cut around the outside lines of the spider.

⑥ Turn the spider over and use the pen to draw eight eyes on its head and a curved line between the two body parts. The spider has two body parts. The part with eyes is called the cephalothorax and the other part is called the abdomen.

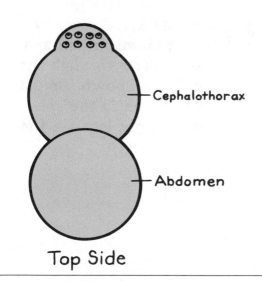

Cephalothorax

Abdomen

Top Side

7 Use the paper punch to make four holes on each side of the cephalothorax, as shown in the picture.

8 ADULT STEP Cut the craft stems in half and stick them through the holes as shown. Adjust the stems so the spider's eight legs are the same length.

9 On the underside, place a piece of tape across the stems to hold them in place.

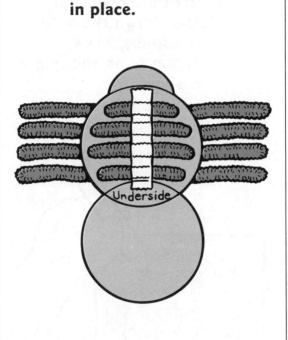

Underside

10 Bend the stems to form eight legs. Keep the spider for the next experiment.

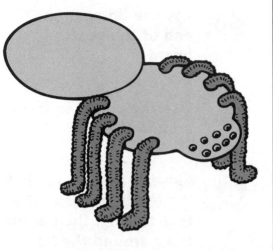

So Now We Know

You can tell from the number of body parts and legs that spiders are not insects. Insects have three main body parts and six legs. Spiders have two main body parts and eight legs.

More Fun Things to Know and Do

Spiders make silk threads. These threads come from holes on the underside of the spider's abdomen. Most spiders have a cord of silk called a dragline trailing behind them. Spiders can use the dragline to gently drop to the ground or turn around and climb back up. Here's how you can show that a dragline protects a spider:

- Take the spider from the original experiment and tape one end of the thread to one end of the underside of the spider's abdomen. The thread is your spider's dragline.

- Tape the free end of the dragline to the edge of a table.

- Move the spider around on the table, then push it off the edge. The dragline keeps the spider from falling to the floor. A real spider could climb up its dragline and get back on the table.

Spiderlings

Round Up These Things

coffee can lid
file folder
pencil
scissors
ruler
pen
paper fastener

Later You'll Need

scissors
ruler
sewing thread
typing paper
school glue

1 Lay the coffee can lid on the file folder.

 2 Use the pencil to trace around the lid.

3 **ADULT STEP** Cut out the circle, cutting through both layers of the file folder.

4 Use the ruler and the pencil to draw two lines on each of the paper circles. The lines must cross and divide the circles into four equal parts.

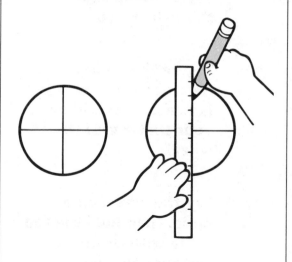

5 **ADULT STEP** On one of the paper circles, cut away part of one of the four sections as shown.

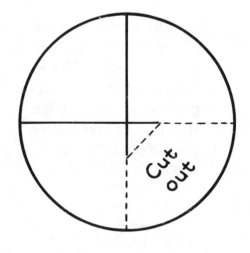

Cut out

6 Turn the paper circle over and print the word SPIDER on the plain side.

Spider

7 On the second paper circle, use the pencil to draw and label the four steps of how a spider grows as shown. Use the pen to trace over your drawings and labels.

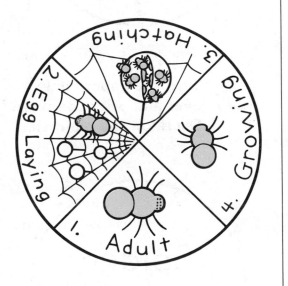

8 ADULT STEP Use the pencil to make a hole through the center of each paper circle.

9 Place the circles together, one on top of the other, so that the cutout opening is on top with the word SPIDER showing. The pictures on the bottom circle should show through the cutout.

10 Secure the circles together with the paper fastener. This will be your spider growth wheel.

11 Lay the wheel on a table, then hold the top circle with one hand and turn the bottom circle counterclockwise with the other hand. The four steps are seen in the cutout as the bottom circle turns.

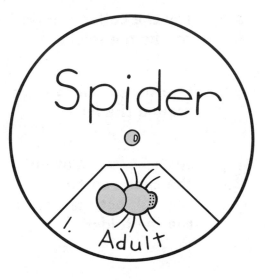

So Now We Know

Spiders come from eggs. They hatch as little spiderlings and grow into adults.

More Fun Things to Know and Do

There are many little spiderlings in most egg sacs. After hatching, a spiderling climbs onto branches, outdoor tables, and other surfaces, then it releases strands of silk. These silk strands and the attached spiderling are lifted by the wind and float to a new area. This is called ballooning and most spiders do this. Here's a way to show ballooning by spiderlings:

- ADULT STEP Cut 3 pieces of thread, each about 6 inches (15 cm) long.

- Tear a penny-size piece from the typing paper.

- Coat the piece of paper with glue.

- Place one end of each thread on the sticky side of the paper.

- Fold the paper, with the sticky sides together, over the glued ends of the threads. The paper is a spiderling and the threads are its strands of silk.

- Repeat this procedure four times to make five spiderlings in all.

- Lay the spiderlings together on a table.

- Lean toward the table so that your mouth is close to but not touching the spiderlings. Then, blow as hard as you can. Where did your spiderlings land?

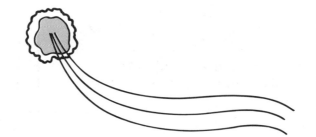

Catchers

Round Up These Things

2-inch (5-cm)-wide transparent tape
10–15 cotton balls
plastic container large enough to hold the cotton balls

Later You'll Need

tape and container of cotton balls from original experiment

Let's find out!

I wonder ... Why are spiderwebs sticky?

ADULT STEP Attach one end of the tape to the center and top of a door frame. Unwind enough tape for the strip to hang about 6 inches (15 cm) from the floor.

 Put the cotton balls in the plastic container.

 Hold the container and stand about 3 feet (0.9 m) from the sticky side of the tape. The tape is a strand from a pretend spiderweb.

4 Throw the cotton balls, one at a time, toward the tape. Count the number that stick to the tape. The balls are pretend insects that get stuck when they fly into a sticky spiderweb.

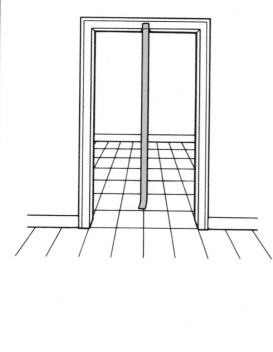

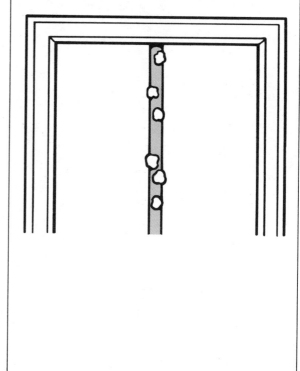

So Now We Know

Spiderwebs are sticky so that they will catch insects for spiders to eat. A spider makes its web sticky with a special liquid silk from its body.

More Fun Things to Know and Do

Spiderwebs come in different shapes and sizes, but they are made of more than one sticky strand. Here's how you can make a pretend spiderweb with many sticky strands:

- Use a doorway with a tiled floor beneath it.

- ADULT STEP   Run a strip of tape from the center of the top of the door frame to the floor. Then run strips of tape diagonally between opposite corners of the door frame.

- Run more strips horizontally and vertically across the doorway, but leave empty spaces between the strips.

- Repeat steps 3 and 4 of the original experiment. Does your larger web catch more insects?

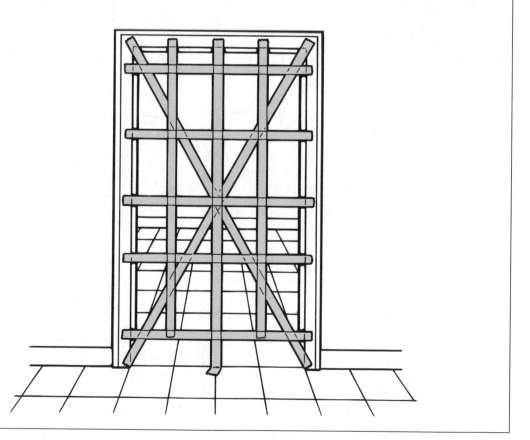

Stuck

I wonder ... Why don't spiders get caught in their own webs?

Let's find out!

Round Up These Things

scissors
ruler
8-inch (20-cm) square of
  stiff paper (A file folder
  works well.)
8-inch (20-cm) square of
  transparent Con-Tact adhesive covering
black permanent marker
4 feet (1.2 m) of yarn

Later You'll Need

spiderweb model made in original
  experiment
several drops of liquid cooking oil
8-inch (20-cm) square of transparent Con-Tact adhesive covering
one-hole paper punch
12-inch (30-cm) piece of yarn
small suction cup hanger

1 **ADULT STEP** Cut a 6-inch (15-cm) square from the center of the stiff paper. Keep the 1-inch (2.5-cm)-wide frame and discard the cutout square.

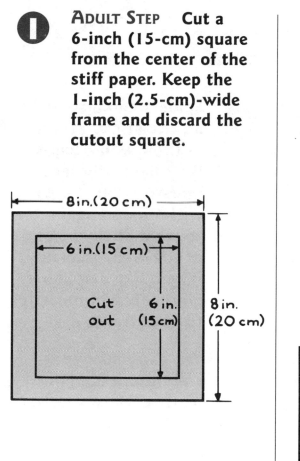

2 **ADULT STEP** Remove the backing from the Con-Tact covering. Lay the Con-Tact covering on a table sticky side up. Lay the frame on the Con-Tact covering and smooth it down.

3 Use the marker to draw a spiderweb on the sticky side of the Con-Tact covering as shown.

4 Cut the yarn into four 1-ft (30-cm) pieces.

5 Lay the yarn pieces across the straight lines of the web.

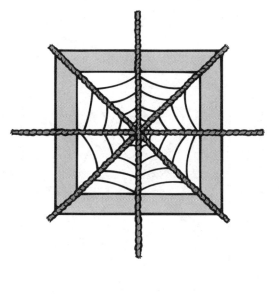

6 Cut off the ends of the yarn that go past the web.

7 With the tip of your pointer finger, touch the strands of the web that are covered with yarn. Your finger does not stick to the yarn-covered strands.

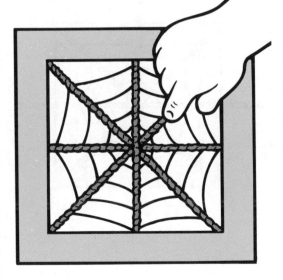

8 With the tip of your pointer finger, touch one of the strands of the web that is not covered with yarn. Your finger sticks to the strand.

So Now We Know

Some of the strands that a spider weaves when building its web are not sticky. The spider can walk on these without getting stuck.

More Fun Things to Know and Do

1 Spiders can also walk on the sticky strands in their web because they have oily feet. Moisten your finger with oil and again touch a sticky strand of the web. Your oily finger, like a spider's oily feet, will not stick to the strand.

2 You can make your web into a hanging picture. Here's how:

• ADULT STEP   Cover the sticky side of the web with another square of Con-Tact covering.

- Make two holes in the top of the frame with the paper punch.

- Thread the yarn through the holes in the frame and tie the ends together on the back of the frame so the knot does not show.

- Secure the suction cup hanger to a windowpane.

- Hang the web on the hanger.

Appendix
Section Summaries

Collecting

The term **bug** is often loosely used to mean any creepy-crawly, including spiders and insects. In the experiment "I.D." (pages 6–9), children learn about the identifying characteristics of an **insect:** three body parts (the **head** [front part], the **thorax** [middle part], and the **abdomen** [hind part]), and six legs, which are attached to the thorax.

In the experiment "Trapper" (pages 10–13), children are shown a safe technique for catching insects. Ways of studying insects are also discovered. The experiment "Sweeper" (pages 14–17) gives safe techniques for catching flying insects. Be sure the children do not try to catch insects that sting, such as bees or wasps. If these are accidentally caught, *do not touch* them with your hands. In fact, unless you are sure that the bug is harmless, do not touch any bug.

In the experiment "Butterfly House" (pages 18–21), children construct a temporary home for butterflies. Children also learn how to catch butterflies. A home for crickets is constructed in the experiment "Bug House" (pages 22–25). Children also discover how to tell boy and girl crickets apart.

Ants are insects that live in **colonies** (groups of the same kind of animal living together). Somewhat like a city, each colony contains hundreds or even thousands of ants. Within a colony live several different kinds of ants: one or more **queen ants** (the "mother" ant that spends her long life of up to 10 to 15 years laying eggs), **male ants** (usually winged ants that function only to mate with the queen during their short life of a few weeks and die soon after mating), and **worker ants** (females that do not mate or lay eggs, but work during their life of 5 to 7 years). Queen ants are larger than the other ants. They usually do not have wings. Males, found only during certain periods of the year, are winged and vary in size, but are always smaller than the queen. In the experiment "Tunnels" (pages 26–29), children learn about the structure of an ant colony from making a model of an ant nest. A **nest** is a place where some bugs lay eggs and raise their young. Children also catch pretend ants and observe the difference in size of the queen and worker ants.

Changing

The changes insects go through during their life cycle is called **metamorphosis.** The number of changes varies with the insect. Some insects, such as the butterfly, undergo **complete metamorphosis,** which means there are four stages: egg, larva, pupa, and adult. In the metamorphosis of a butterfly, the **larva** (the second stage of complete metamorphosis) is called a **caterpillar**, and the **pupa** (the third, resting stage of complete metamorphosis) is called a **chrysalis.** Some other insects, such as the grasshopper, undergo **incomplete metamorphosis,** which means there are three stages of development: egg, nymph, and adult. A **nymph** is a smaller version of the adult. If the adult has wings, the wings develop during the nymph stage. In the experiment "Around and Around" (pages 32–35), children make models to demonstrate both complete and incomplete metamorphosis.

The firm outside covering of an insect or spider is called an **exoskeleton.** The exoskeleton does not grow as the insect larvae and nymphs grow. Insects in these stages and growing spiders shed their exoskeletons as they grow. This is called **molting.** Generally, adult insects and spiders do not grow. In the experiment "Break Out" (pages 36–39), children experience how a grasshopper nymph breaks out of its exoskeleton and how a butterfly breaks out of its chrysalis.

Moving

All caterpillars are not alike, but they have the same basic body structure, with up to thirteen segments and a head with six simple eyes on each side. They have six "true" legs on the first three body segments. These true legs are generally longer and thinner than the five pairs of shorter, fatter, "false" legs on the middle and four end segments. The true legs become the legs of the adult moth or butterfly that the caterpillar changes into. The ten false legs are used to support and move the growing body of the caterpillar. On the bottom of the false legs, small hooks called **crochets** act as grippers, allowing the caterpillar to hold tightly on to a branch or leaf. The false legs are shed when the caterpillar loses its last skin. In the experiment "Creepers" (pages 42–45), children make a model of the basic body structure of a caterpillar and use it to show how a caterpillar creeps along. Some caterpillars, called loopers or inchworms, have fewer false legs in the middle segment. The false legs on the end inch forward and the middle segment loops upward. The name looper or inchworm comes from this movement.

Bugs on land move from place to place by walking on legs. The number of legs varies: centipedes have twenty-six or more legs, spiders eight, and insects six. The fewer and longer the legs are, the harder it is for the animal to balance. A centipede can lift many legs without falling over. In the experiment "Lifters" (pages 46–49), children discover that insects must balance and walk on three legs, which must be the front and hind legs on one side, plus the middle leg on the opposite side.

The legs of insects have four main parts. Tiny hairs on the ends of their jointed legs are moist with a sticky liquid. The ends of the moist hairs wet the surface the insects are walking on, then stick to the surface. This allows insects to walk upside down on ceilings. In the experiment "Sticky Feet" (pages 50–53), children make a model insect leg, wet it, and stick it to a surface so it hangs upside down. Children also use a mirror to experience the feeling of walking upside down.

The tendency of molecules of a liquid, such as water, to cling together at the surface to form a skinlike film is called **surface tension.** Because water has surface tension, lightweight bugs can walk across the surface without sinking. In the experiment "Water Walkers" (pages 54–57), children make models of bugs that can stand on water.

Damselflies generally have narrower wings and thinner bodies than dragonflies. One identifying characteristic is that dragonflies rest with their wings straight out, whereas damselflies hold their wings together above their backs. Both of these insects fly very fast. In the experiment "Speedy" (pages 58–61), children make models of dragonflies and damselflies.

During forward flight, the wings of insects move in a figure-eight pattern. The effect of this motion is to draw air from above and in front of the insect and push it backward over the top of the insect. Faster-moving air pushes less against an object it passes by than does slower-moving air. This creates regions of low pressure above and in front of the insect. The difference in the pressure above and below the insect produces an upward force called **lift,** which raises the insect and keeps it in the air. The difference in the pressure in front of and behind the insect produces forward movement. The experiment "Flutter" (pages 62–65) shows how moving air causes lift. This experiment also shows how touching a butterfly's wing can lift scales on the wing, interfering with airflow and making it difficult for the butterfly to fly.

Fleas are able to jump high because their back legs are long and strong, and have in them a special elastic protein called **resilin.** When a flea bends its legs to begin a jump, the resilin compresses like a spring. When the flea stretches its legs, the resilin springs back to its normal shape. This change catapults the flea upward through the air. In the experiment "Springy" (pages 66–68), children make a paper model of a flea and use various styles of models to stage a flea Olympics.

Communicating

Some bees communicate among themselves by dancing. A female bee that finds a rich supply of nectar returns to the hive and tells the others the location of food supplies by dancing. If the food is close, the bee dances in a circle. If the food is far away, she does the **waggle** dance, which consists of quick movements from side to side down the center line of a figure-eight pattern. The more distant the food, the faster she waggles. In the experiment "Dancers" (pages 70–73), children learn to do the waggle dance and imitate how the rapidity of a bee's waggle tells the other bees how far away the food is.

Fireflies give off light because of chemical changes inside their abdomens. One change turns the light on, and a second change turns it off. The lighted area usually is on the side of the abdomen. The male firefly finds the female by following her flashing lights. Unlike the light from fires and lightbulbs, the light made by fireflies is cool to the touch. The production of light by living things is called **bioluminescence.** In the experiment "Flashers" (pages 74–77), a light stick is used to represent a firefly's light and to make a model of a firefly.

Eating

Insects do not have teeth. A grasshopper is able to chew by grinding its ridged jaws together, whereas a fly eats only liquid through a **proboscis,** a feeding tube that uncoils and is used like a straw. In the experiment "Munchers" (pages 80–83), children discover how grasshoppers and flies eat.

Butterflies eat only nectar and other liquids. They can taste the sweet nectar of flowers with their feet. The taste causes the butterfly to uncoil its proboscis and stick it into the flower to drink. In the experiment "Sippers" (pages 84–86), children use straws to eat like a butterfly and party blowers to see how a proboscis uncoils.

Camouflaging

A **predator** is an animal that hunts and eats other animals. The animal that becomes the meal for the predator is called the **prey.** The colors and/or shape of an animal's body that blend in with its environment are called **camouflage.** In the experiment "Hide-and-Seek" (pages 88–91), children make a model of a walkingstick and other bugs, and use them to demonstrate camouflage.

Many butterflies have wings that are brightly colored on the top side to attract a mate. But generally the reverse side has a dull color with a more confusing pattern that helps to hide the butterfly when it is resting. In the experiment "Top and Bottom" (pages 92–95), children make decorative paper butterfly wings to show how their color helps the butterfly to blend in or stand out.

Spinning

Spiders are bugs that have two body parts and eight legs. A spider's two main body parts are called the **cephalothorax** (combined head and thorax) and the abdomen. Its eight legs are attached to the cephalothorax. A spider generally has eight eyes located on the top and front of its head. The spider releases **silk,** which is a protein that can be pulled from the spider's body by fingerlike parts on the underside of its abdomen called **spinnerets.** In the experiment "Over the Edge" (pages 98–101), children make a model of a spider and learn how a **dragline** (a cord, generally made of two thick strands of silk, by which a spider can suspend itself) protects the spider from falling. When a real spider climbs up its dragline, the dragline disappears as the spider climbs. This is because the spider catches the cord on one of its legs and rolls the silk into a ball as it climbs. The ball is dropped or eaten by the spider.

Unlike insects, spiders undergo very little metamorphosis during their development. The adult generally lays eggs in a silken sac, which may be put in all sorts of places. Some egg sacs are placed in or near the web, and some are carried by the female. The eggs usually hatch in a few weeks. The **spiderlings** (young spiders) usually cut or tear open the egg sac with their jaws and fangs. Spiderlings that hatch during cool fall weather may stay in the sac until warm spring weather arrives. In the experiment "Spiderlings" (pages 102–105), children discover the steps of spider development and find out about the technique that spiderlings use to float through the air and move to new areas. This technique is called **ballooning.**

Spiderwebs are constructed with silk made inside a spider's body. On the hind end of the spider's abdomen are pointed bumps called spinnerets. Liquid from inside the spider flows out of the spinnerets, which spins the liquid silk strands. One kind of silk dries in the air and another kind stays sticky. In the experiment "Catchers" (pages 106–109), children discover that a spider adds sticky silk to its web to catch insects for food. An orb web, the most common spiderweb design, is made with spirals of silk strands. In the experiment "Stuck" (pages 110–113), children learn that some of the strands in an orb web are not sticky.

Glossary

abdomen The hind part of a bug's body.

ballooning A technique that spiderlings use to float through the air and move to new areas.

bioluminescence The production of light by living things.

bug A word used in this book to mean any small creepy-crawly, including spiders and insects.

camouflage Colors and/or patterns that conceal an object by matching the background.

caterpillar Butterfly or moth larva.

cephalothorax The combined head and thorax of a spider.

chrysalis Butterfly pupa.

colonies Groups of the same kind of animal living together.

complete metamorphosis Four-staged metamorphosis: egg, larva, pupa, and adult.

crochets Small hooks on the bottom of a caterpillar's false legs which act as grippers, allowing the caterpillar to hold tightly on to a branch or leaf.

dragline A cord, generally made of two thick strands of silk, by which a spider can suspend itself.

exoskeleton The outside covering of the body of an insect or spider.

head The front part of a bug's body.

incomplete metamorphosis Three-staged metamorphosis: egg, nymph, and adult.

insect A bug with three body parts, three pairs of legs, and often one or two pairs of wings.

larva (plural **larvae**) The young wormlike form of an insect during the second stage of complete metamorphosis.

lift An upward force created by difference in the pressure above and below an insect or any flying object, which raises the insect or object and keeps it in the air.

male ants Usually winged ants that function only to mate with the queen during their short life of a few weeks and die soon after mating.

metamorphosis Changes in the life cycle of an insect. See also **complete metamorphosis** and **incomplete metamorphosis.**

molt To shed an exoskeleton.

nest A place used by some bugs to lay eggs and raise their young.

nymph The second stage of incomplete metamorphosis, during which the nymph is smaller than the adult and has no functional wings.

predator An animal that hunts and eats other animals.

prey An animal that is hunted and eaten by another animal.

proboscis The feeding tube of certain insects, such as flies and butterflies.

pupa (plural **pupae**) The third stage of complete metamorphosis between the larva and the adult.

queen ant The "mother" ant that spends her long life of up to 10 to 15 years laying eggs.

resilin Elastic protein.

silk A protein produced by bugs, such as caterpillars and spiders, that can be pulled from the bug's body into smooth, fine, or thick strands.

spider   A bug that has two body parts and four pairs of legs, and that is capable of producing silk from spinnerets.

spiderlings   Young spiders.

spinnerets   The fingerlike body parts located at the end and on the underside of a spider's abdomen, where spiders and certain larvae release silk from their bodies.

surface tension   The tendency of molecules of a liquid, such as water, to cling together to form a skinlike film across the surface of the liquid.

thorax   The middle part of a bug's body.

waggle   Quick movements from side to side.

worker ants   Female ants that do not mate or lay eggs, but work during their life of 5 to 7 years.

Index